Kangaroo
Coloring Book

Get FREE printable coloring pages and discounted book prices sent straight to your e-mail inbox every week!

Sign up at:

www.adultcoloringworld.net

-ADULT COLORING- WORLD

ISBN-13: 978-1542370677
ISBN-10: 1542370671

Previews:

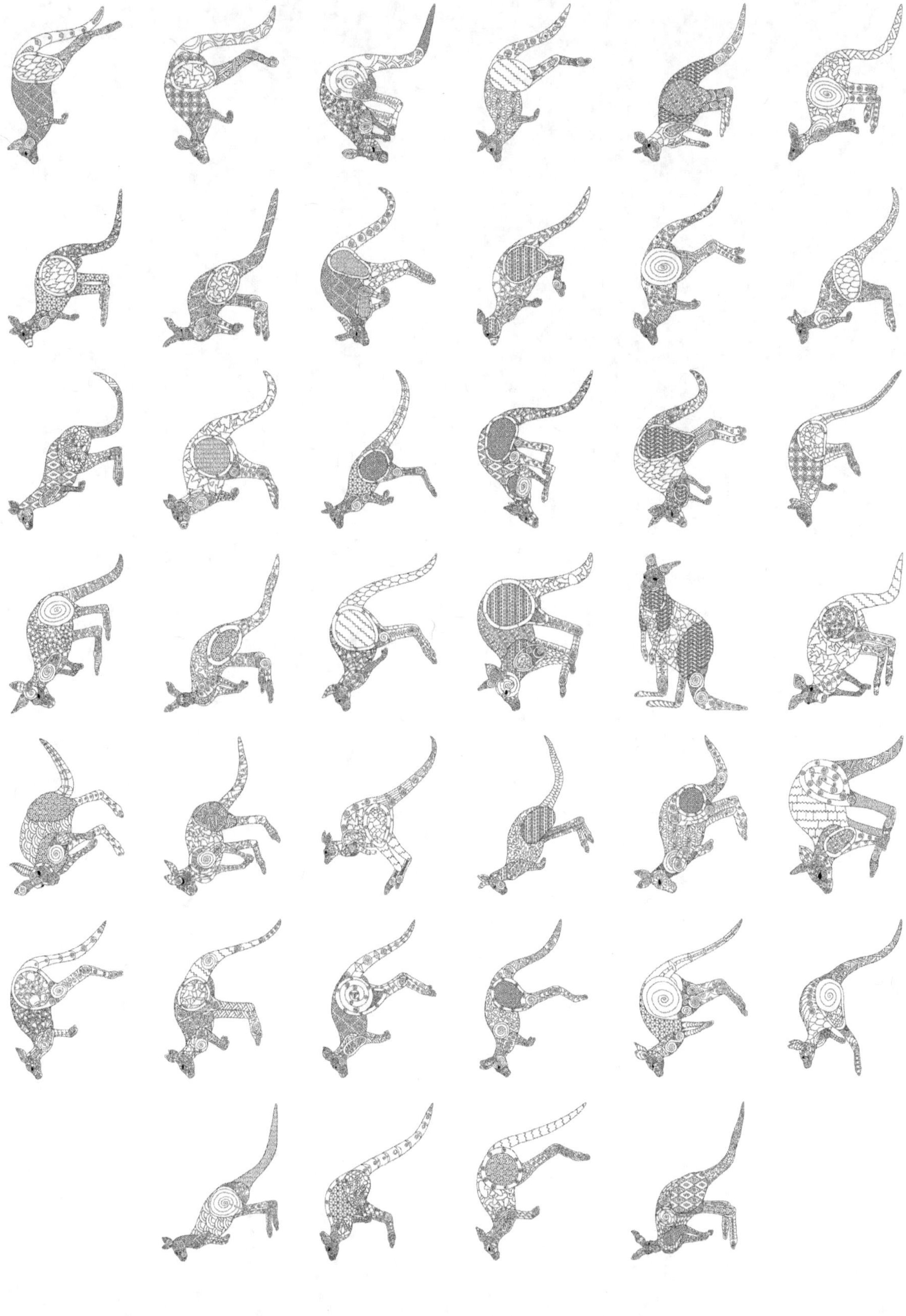

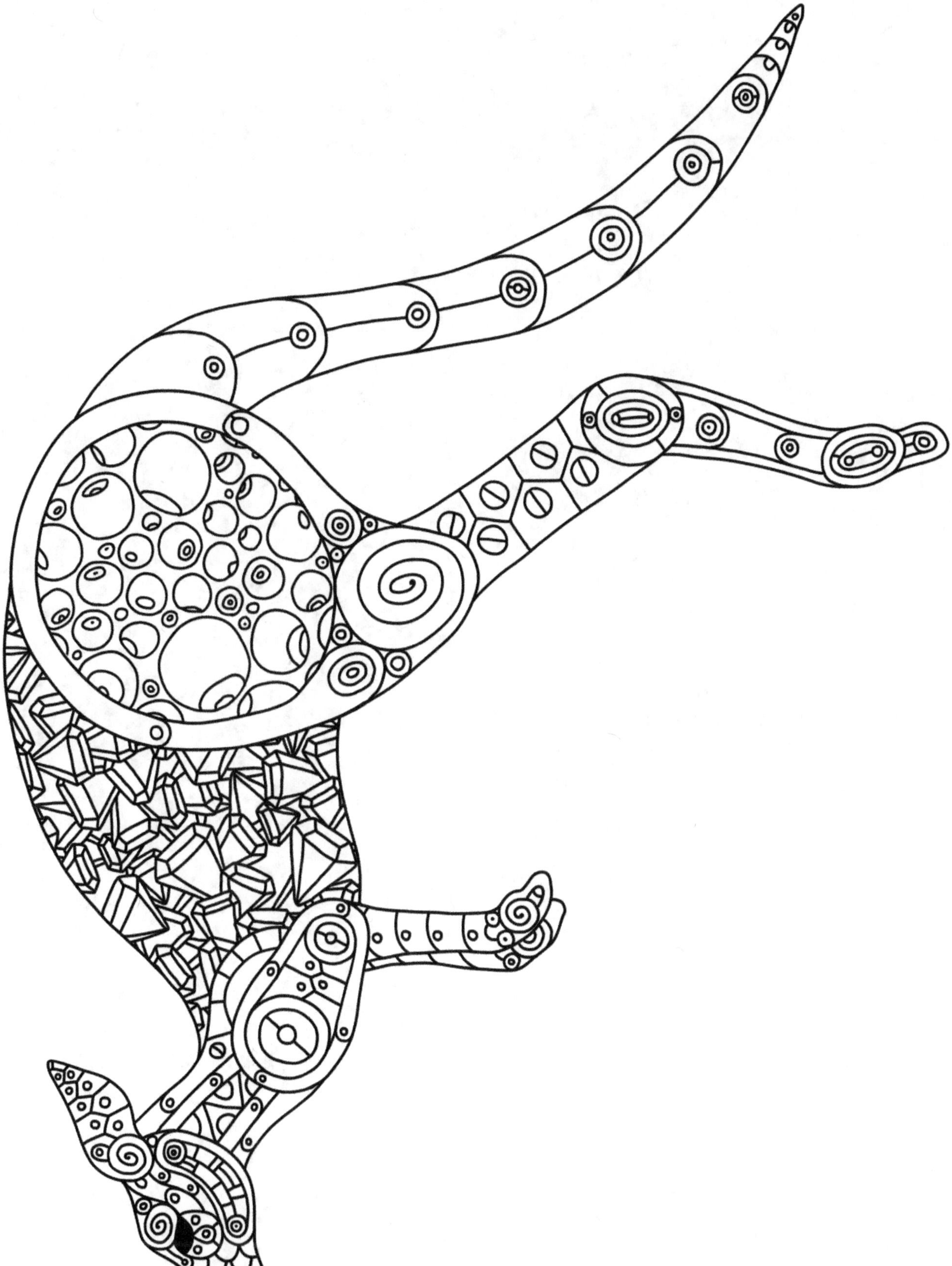

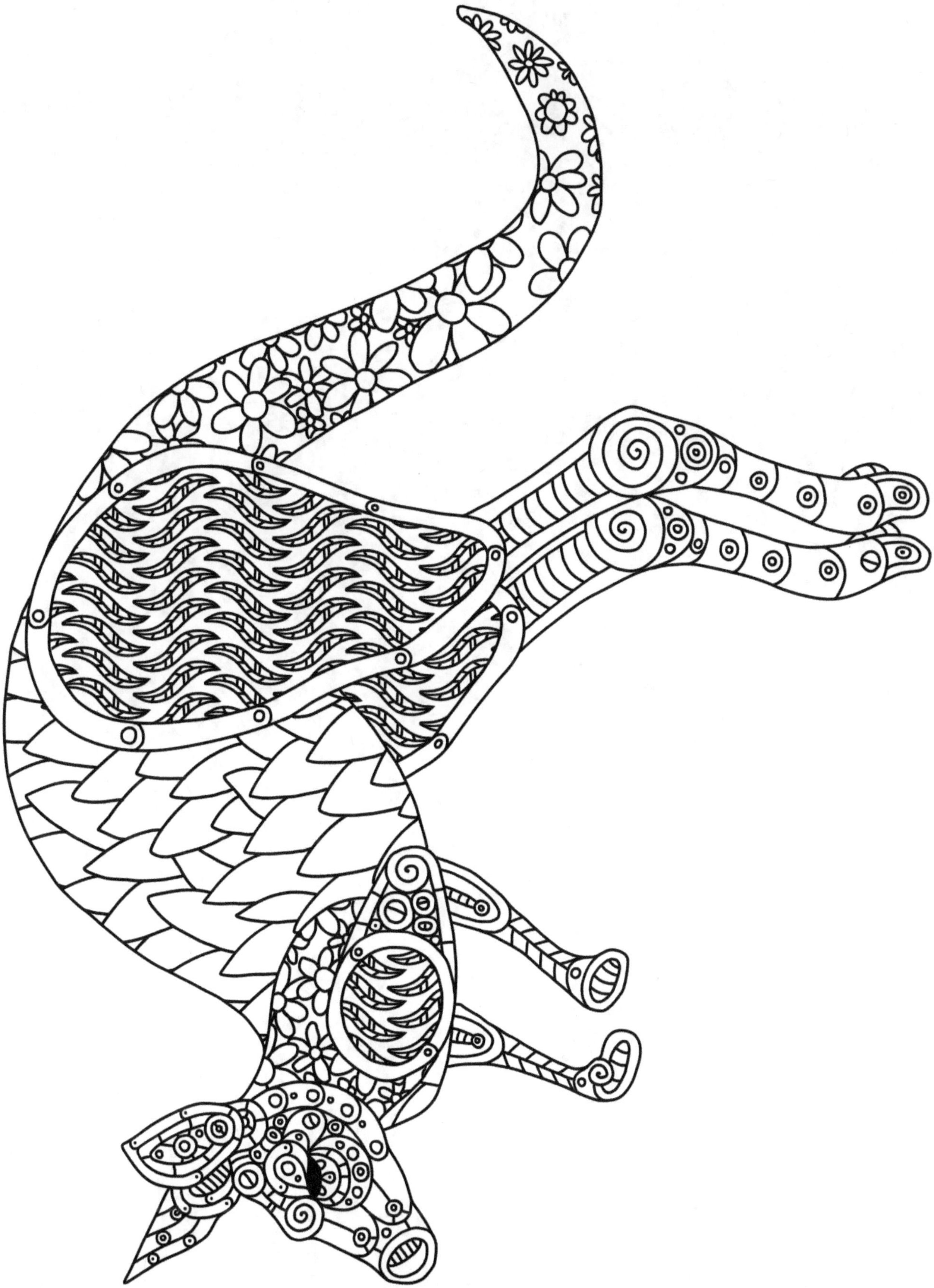

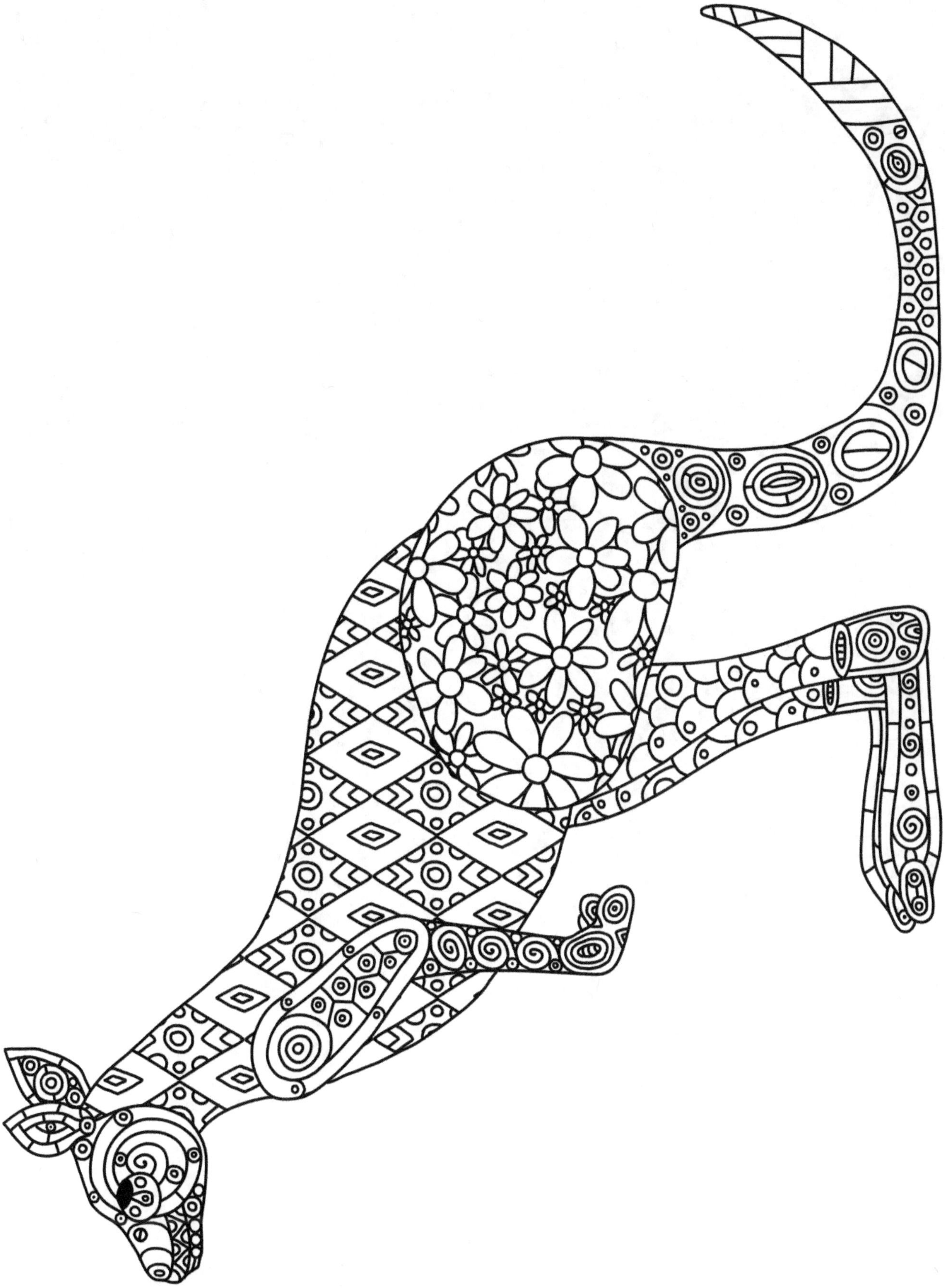

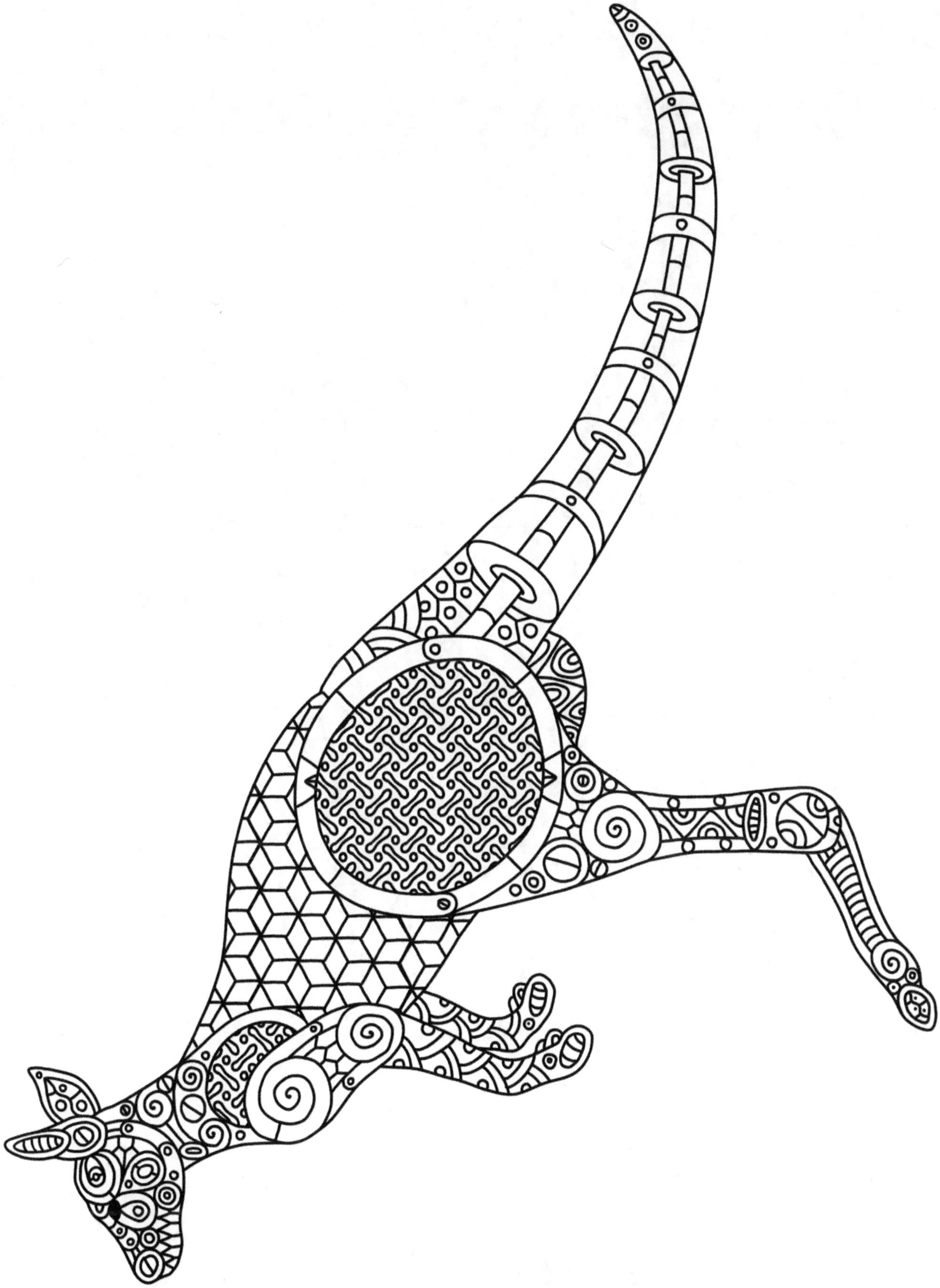

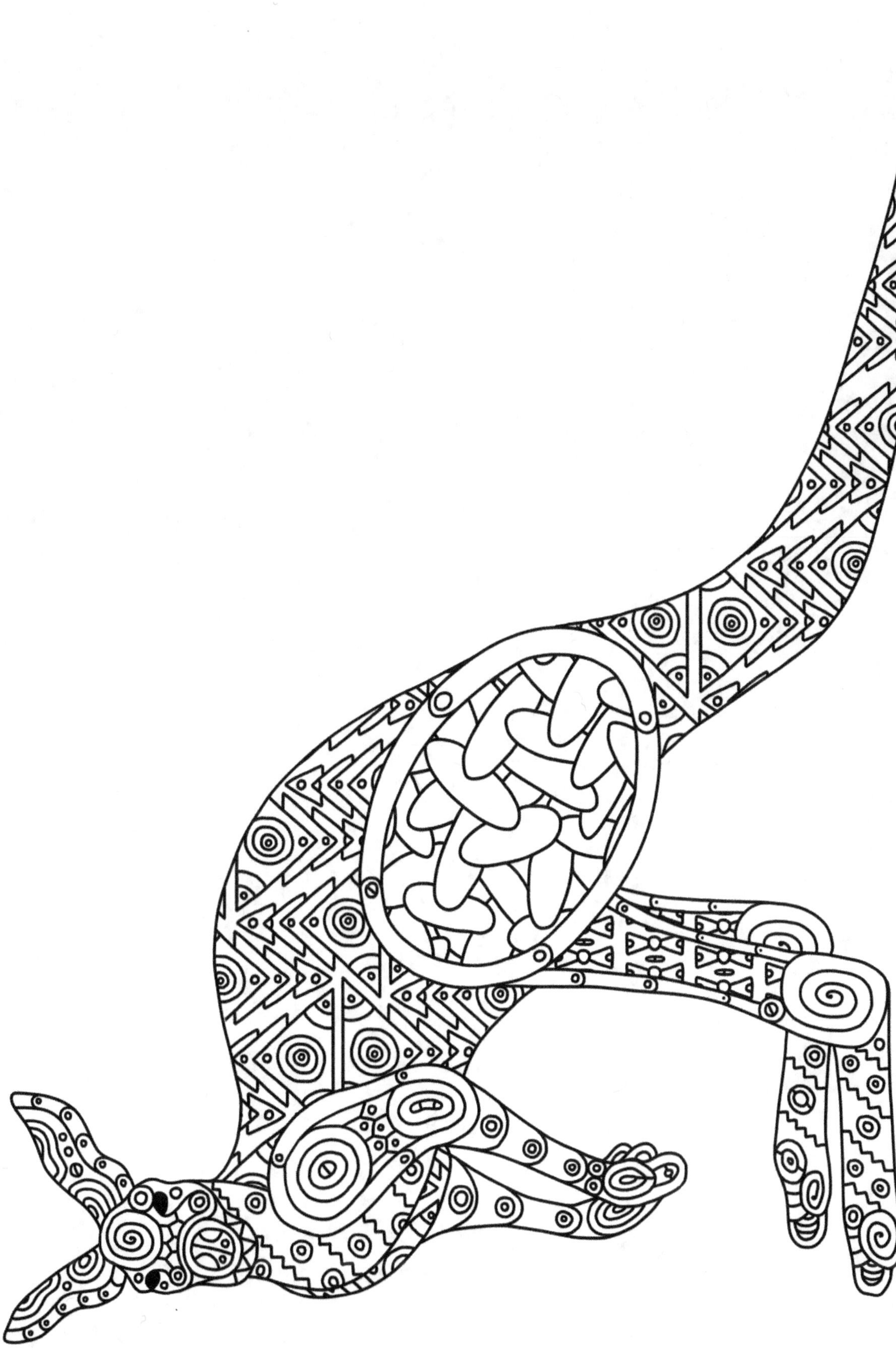

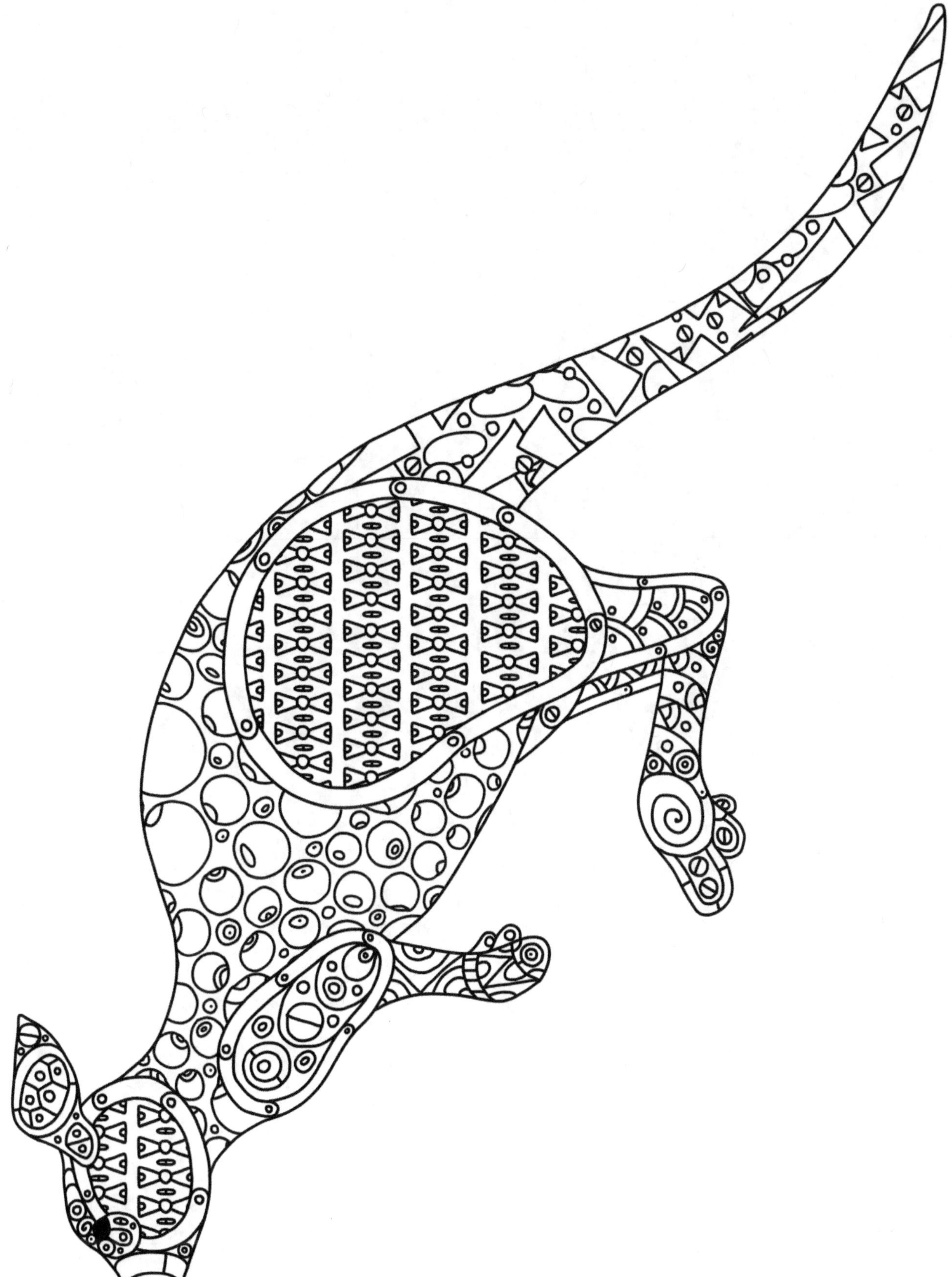

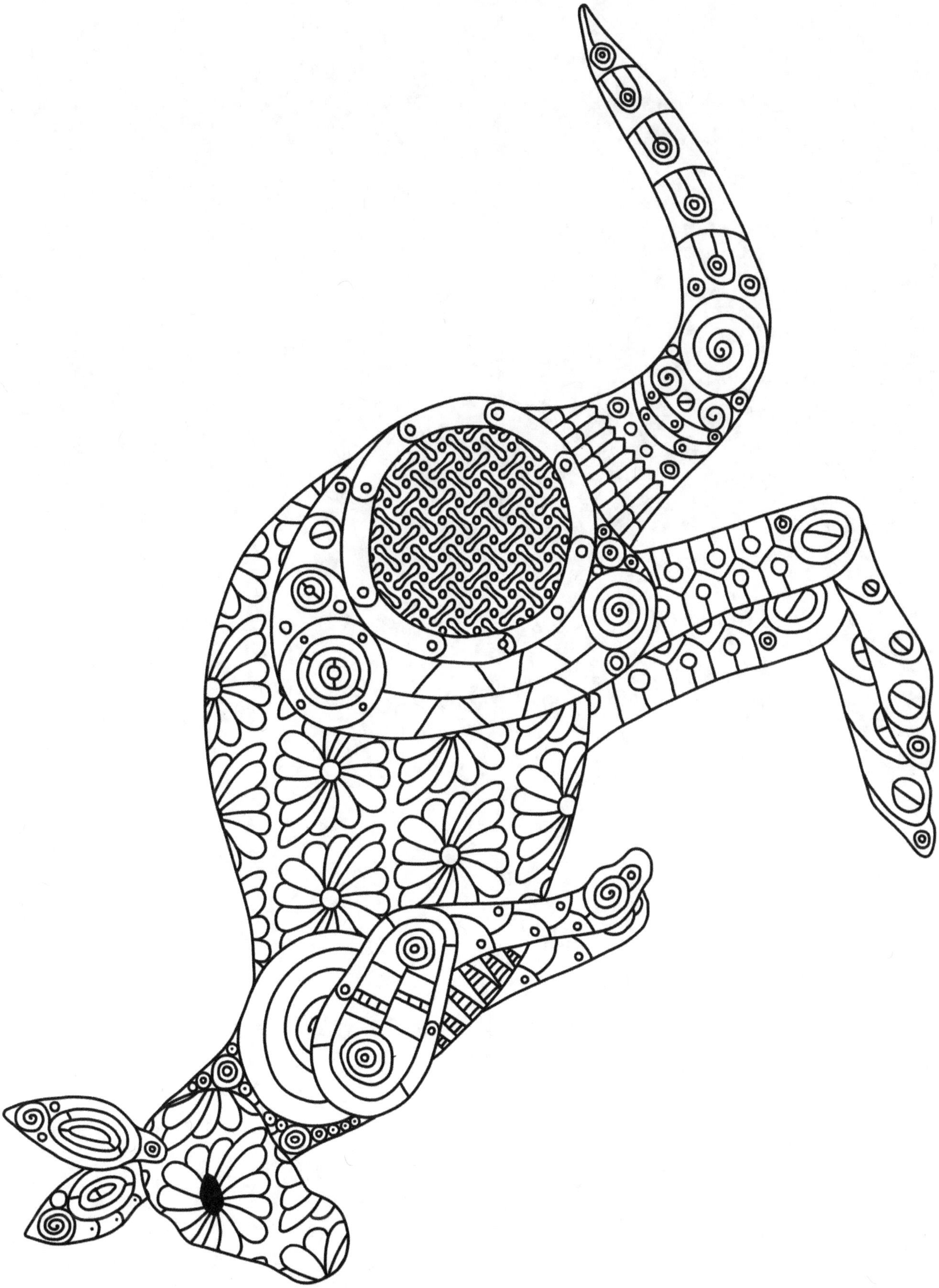

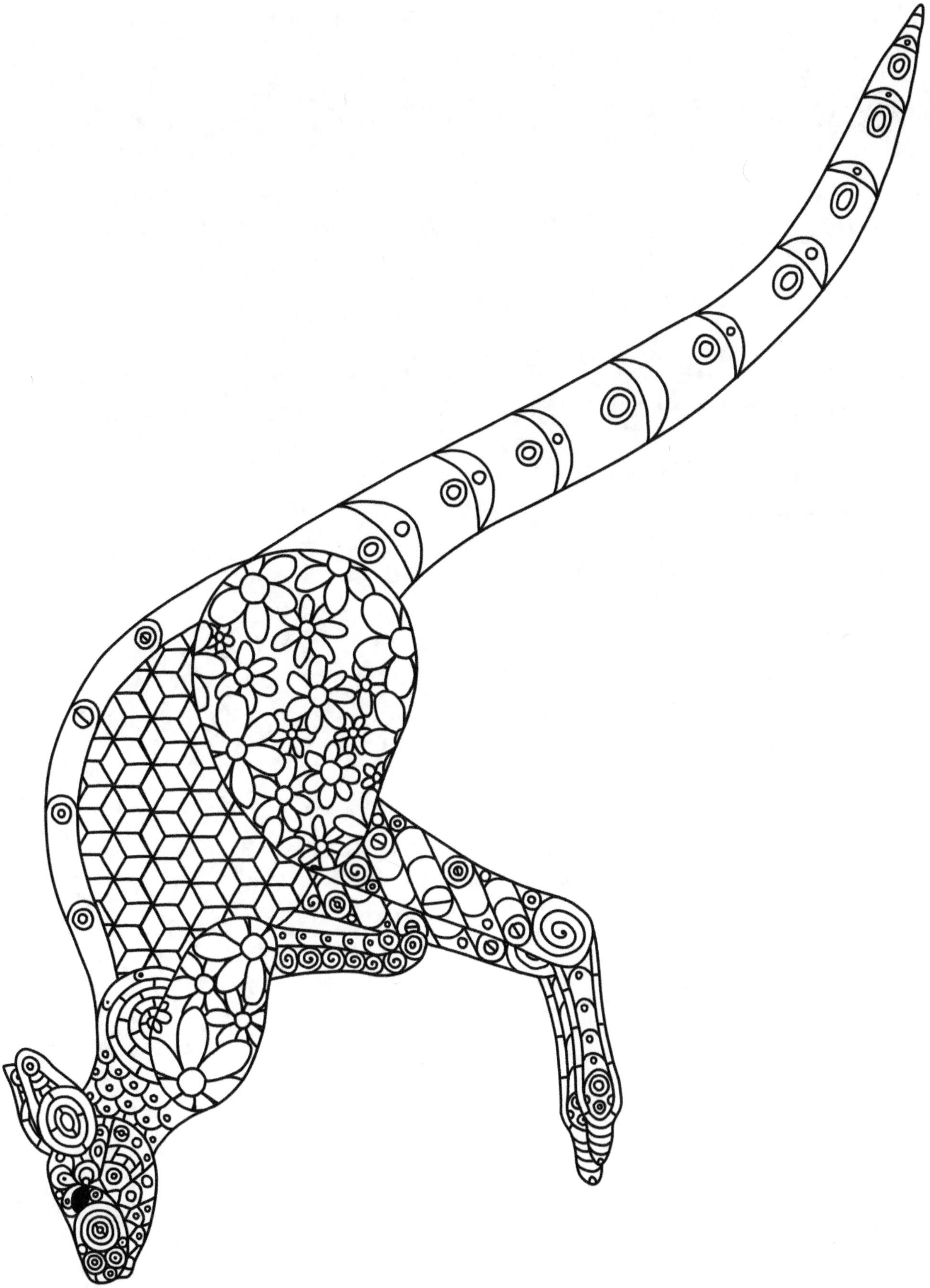

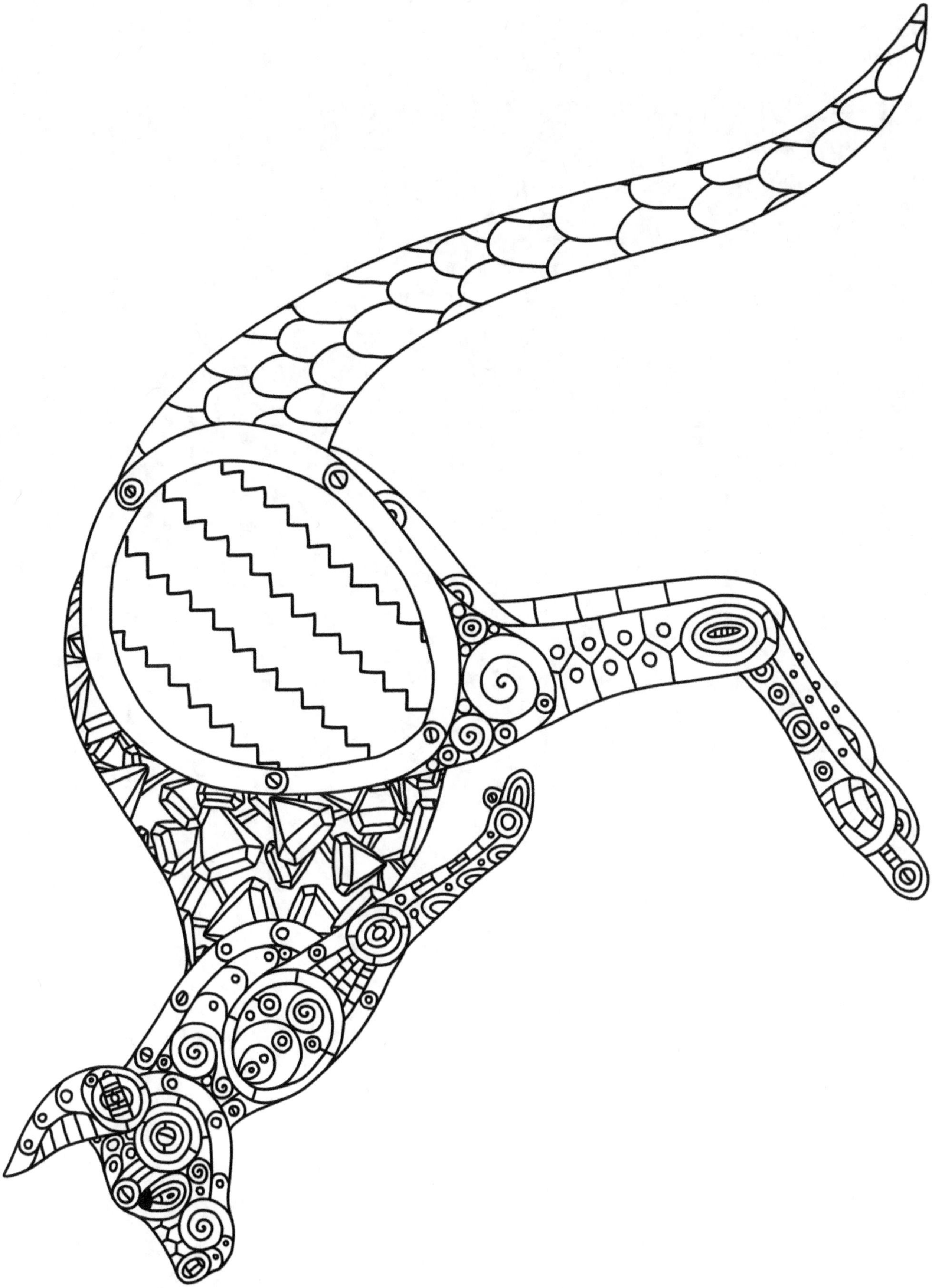

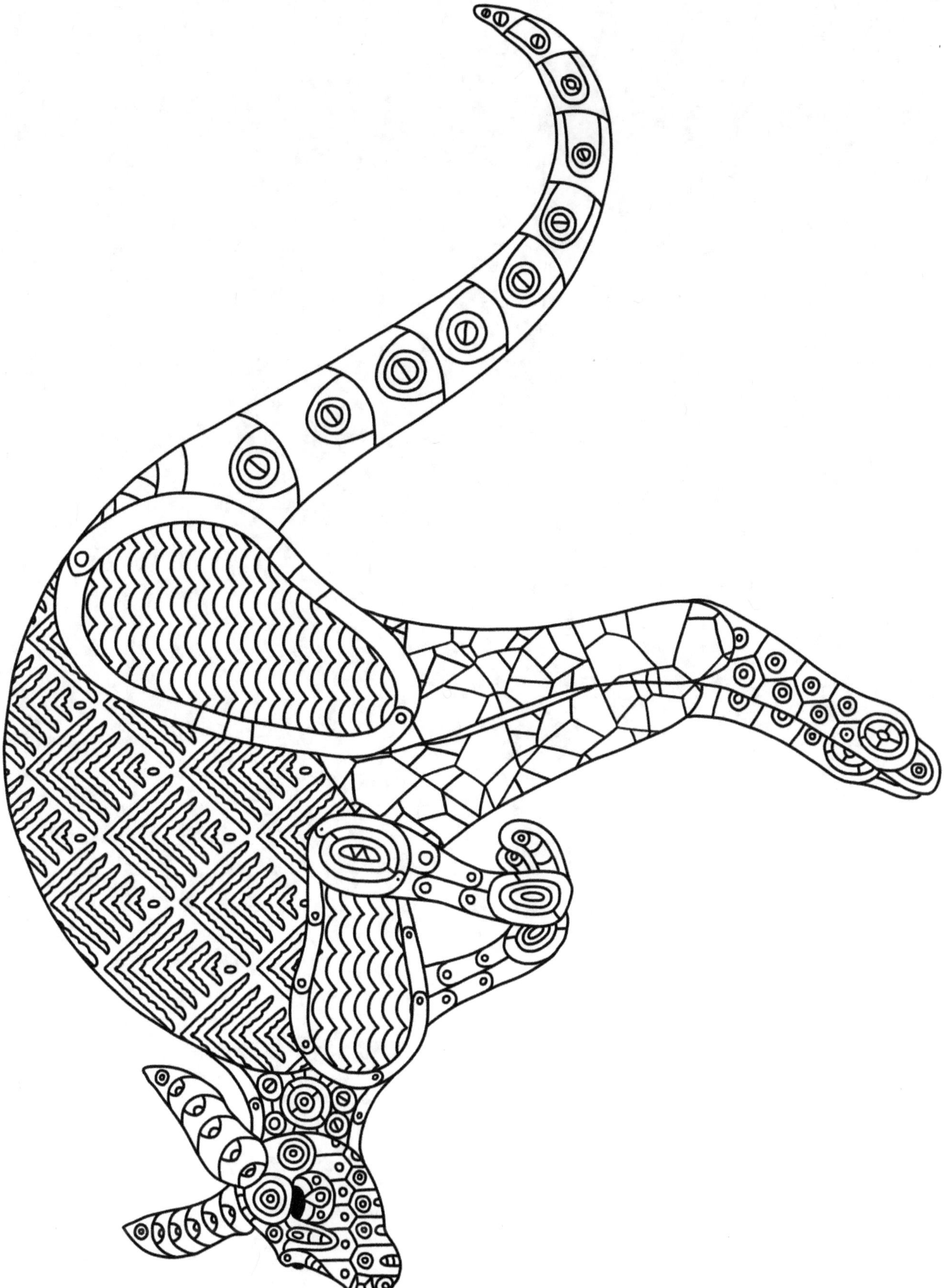

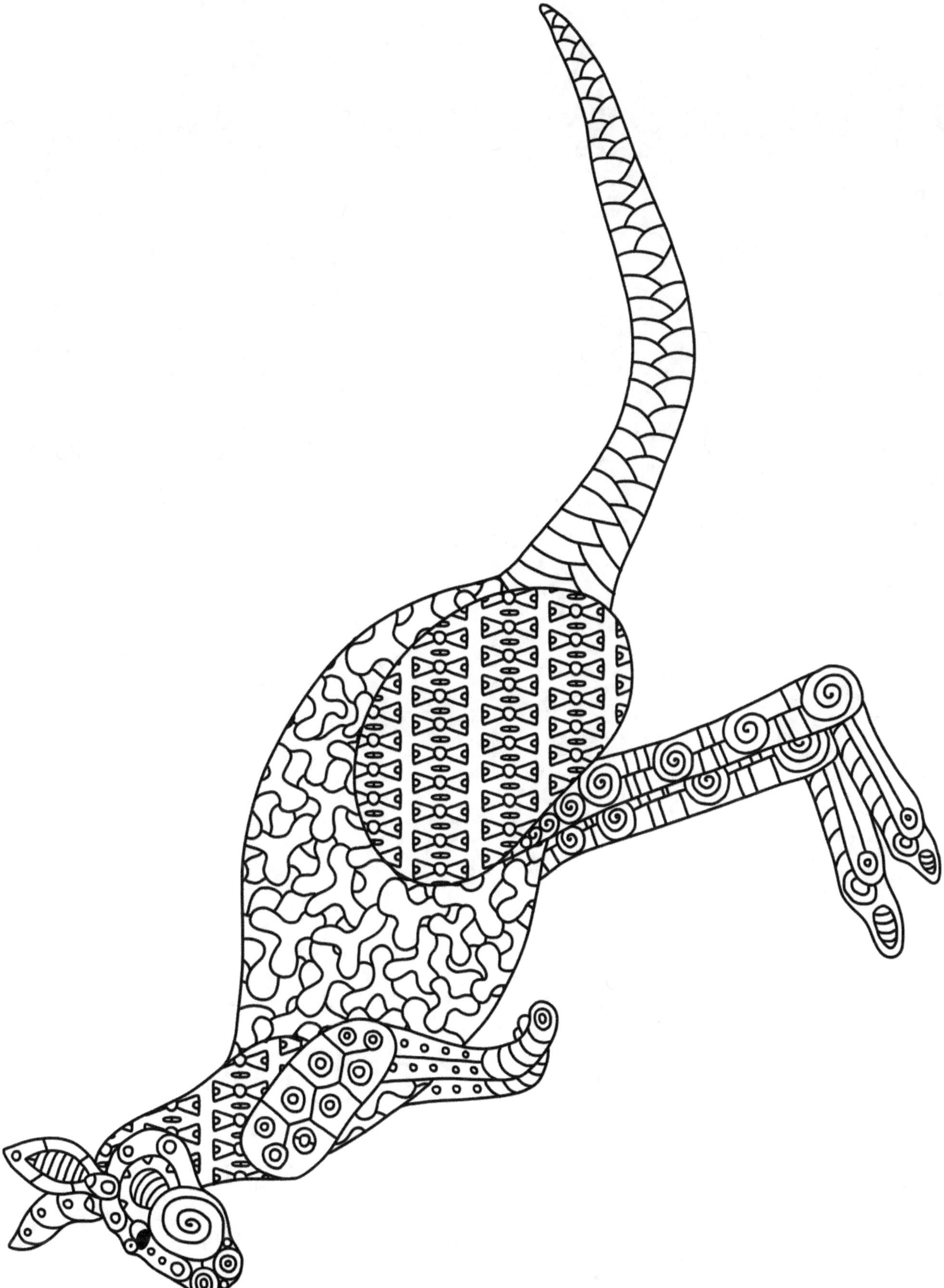

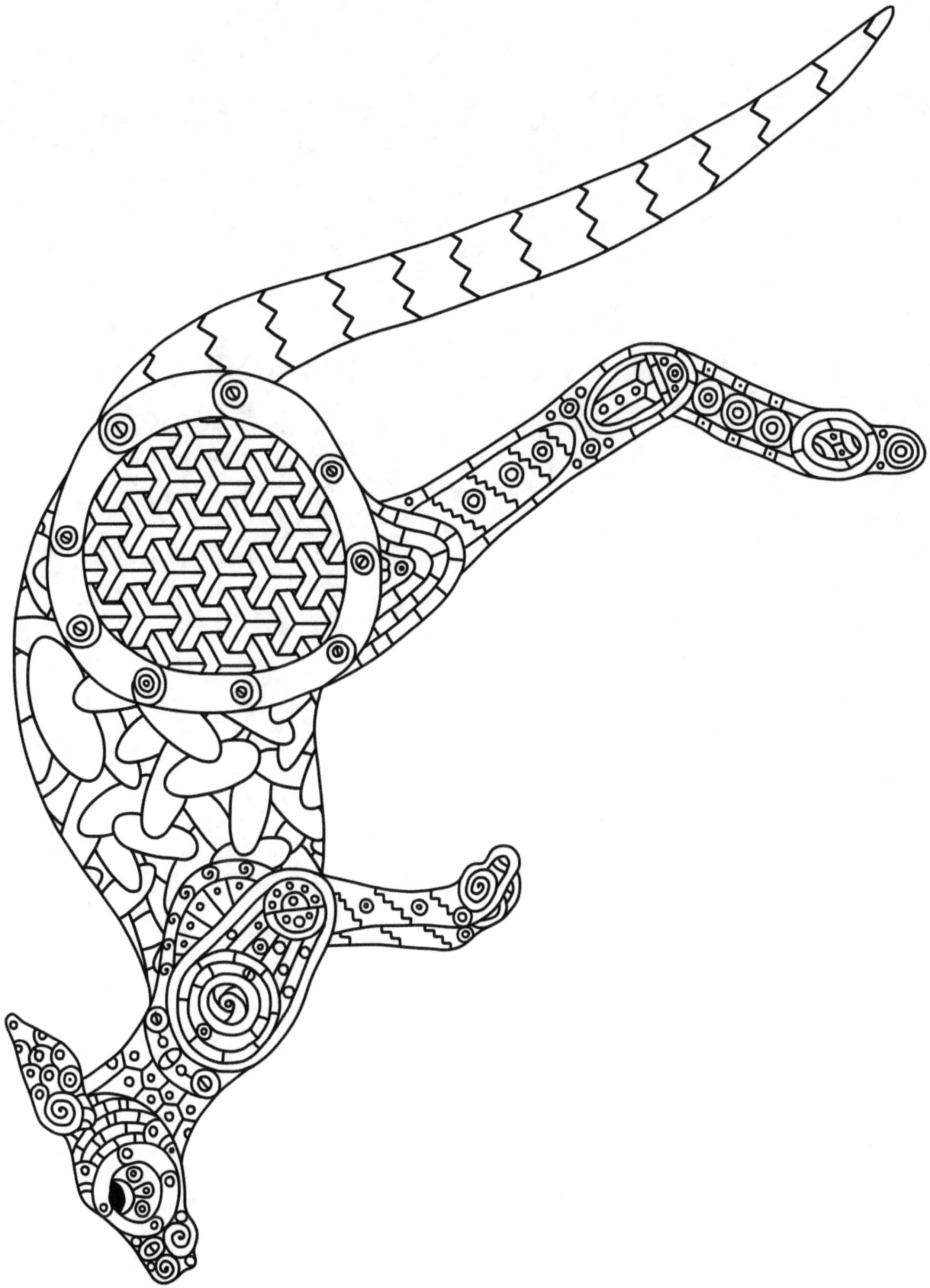

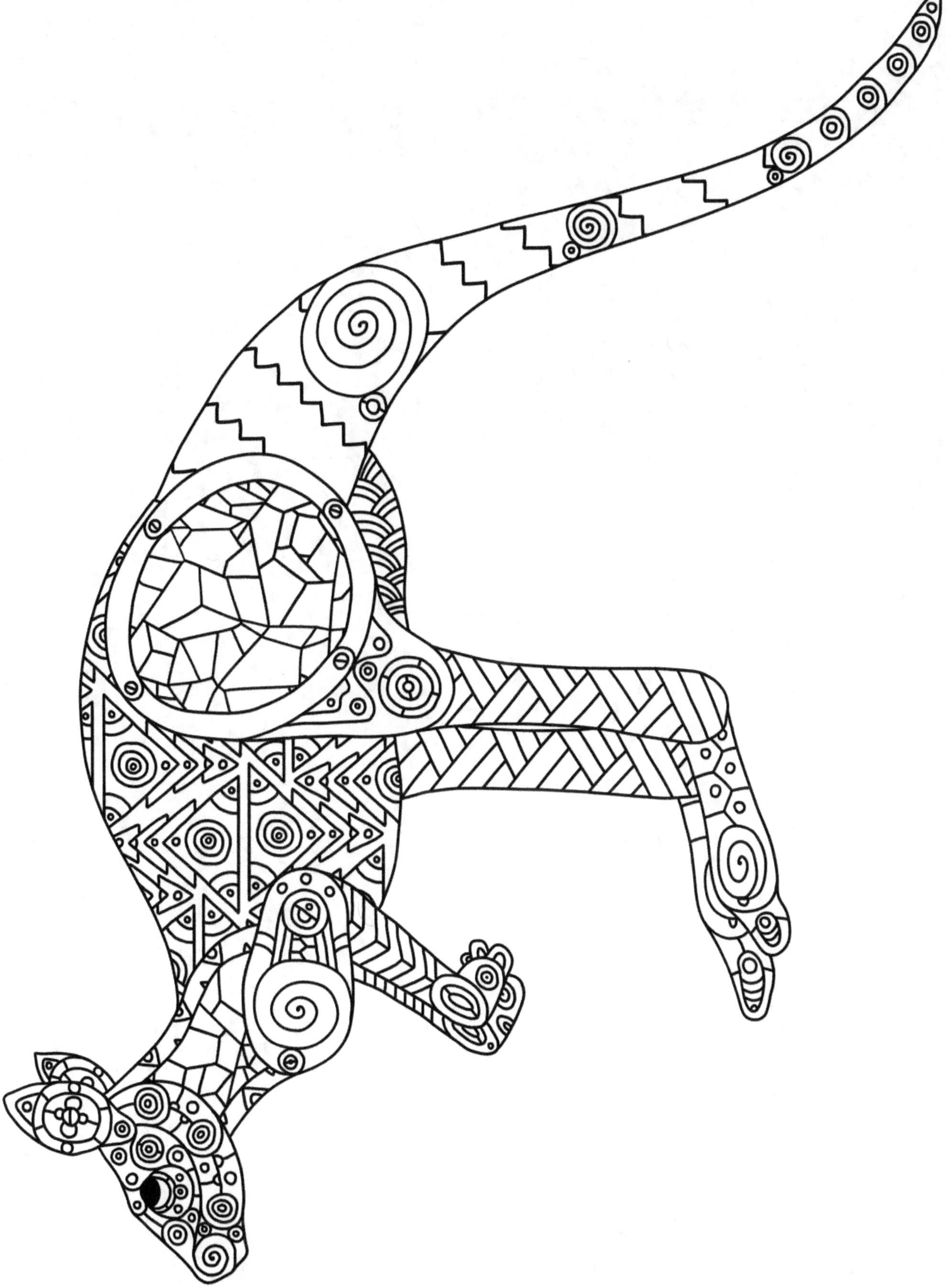

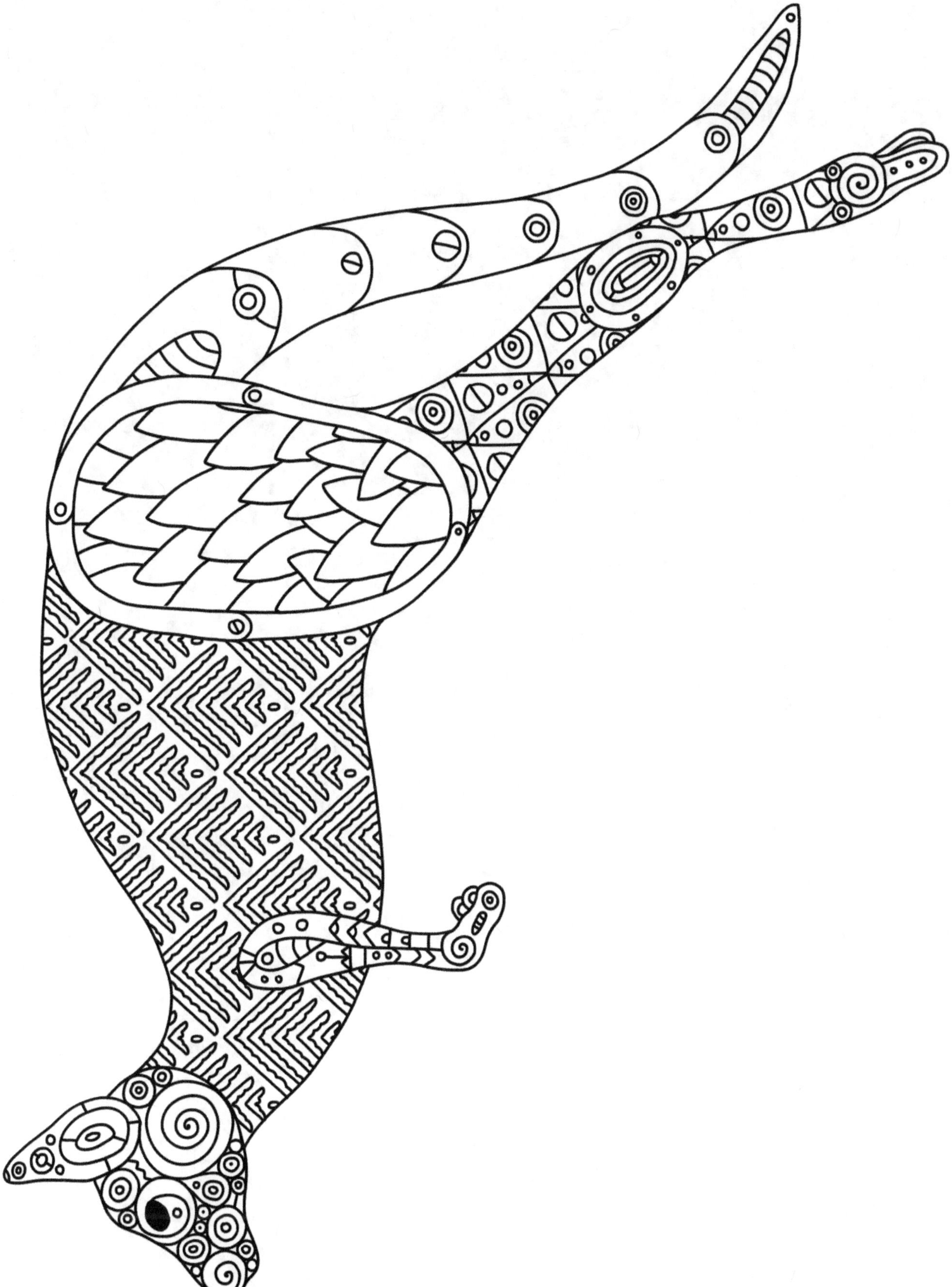

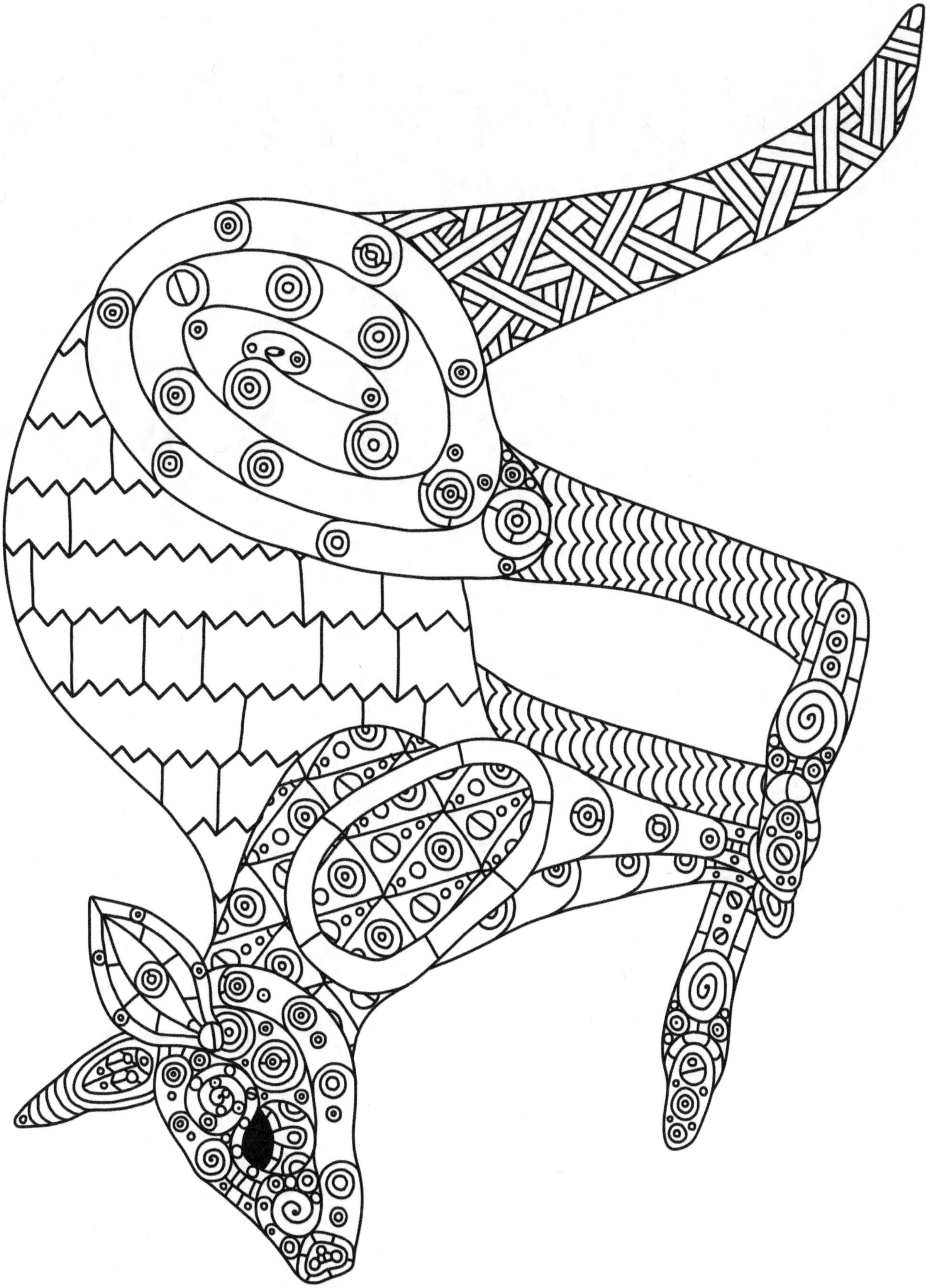

COLOR TEST PAGE

Color Test Page

www.ingramcontent.com/pod-product-compliance
Lightning Source LLC
Chambersburg PA
CBHW051947280526
45789CB00009B/3207
9781542370677